Hi, my name is Milo. I'm going to teach you about computers with ABC's. Come with me and lets get started!!!

Aa

A IS FOR ACCESS

A computer gives you access to the internet.

B IS FOR BACKUP

Bb

You can make a backup copy on a computer.

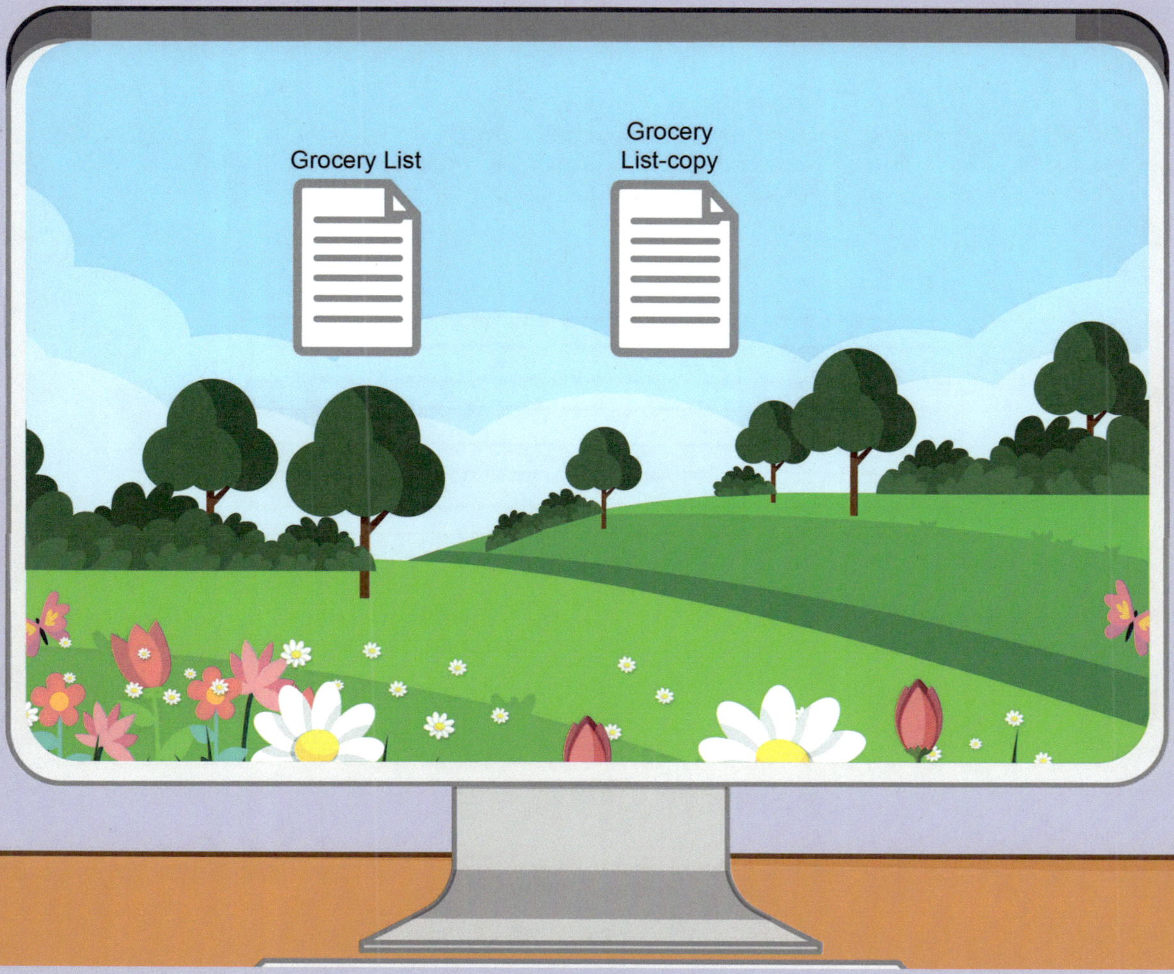

Cc

C IS FOR COMPUTER

You can use a computer to type a document.

D IS FOR DATA

Dd

A computer can store data like emails, phone numbers and photos.

Ee

E IS FOR EMAIL

You can send and recieve emails with a computer.

F IS FOR FILE

Ff

You can attach a photo or another file to an email.

Gg

G IS FOR GRAPHICS

A graphic is an image on a computer.

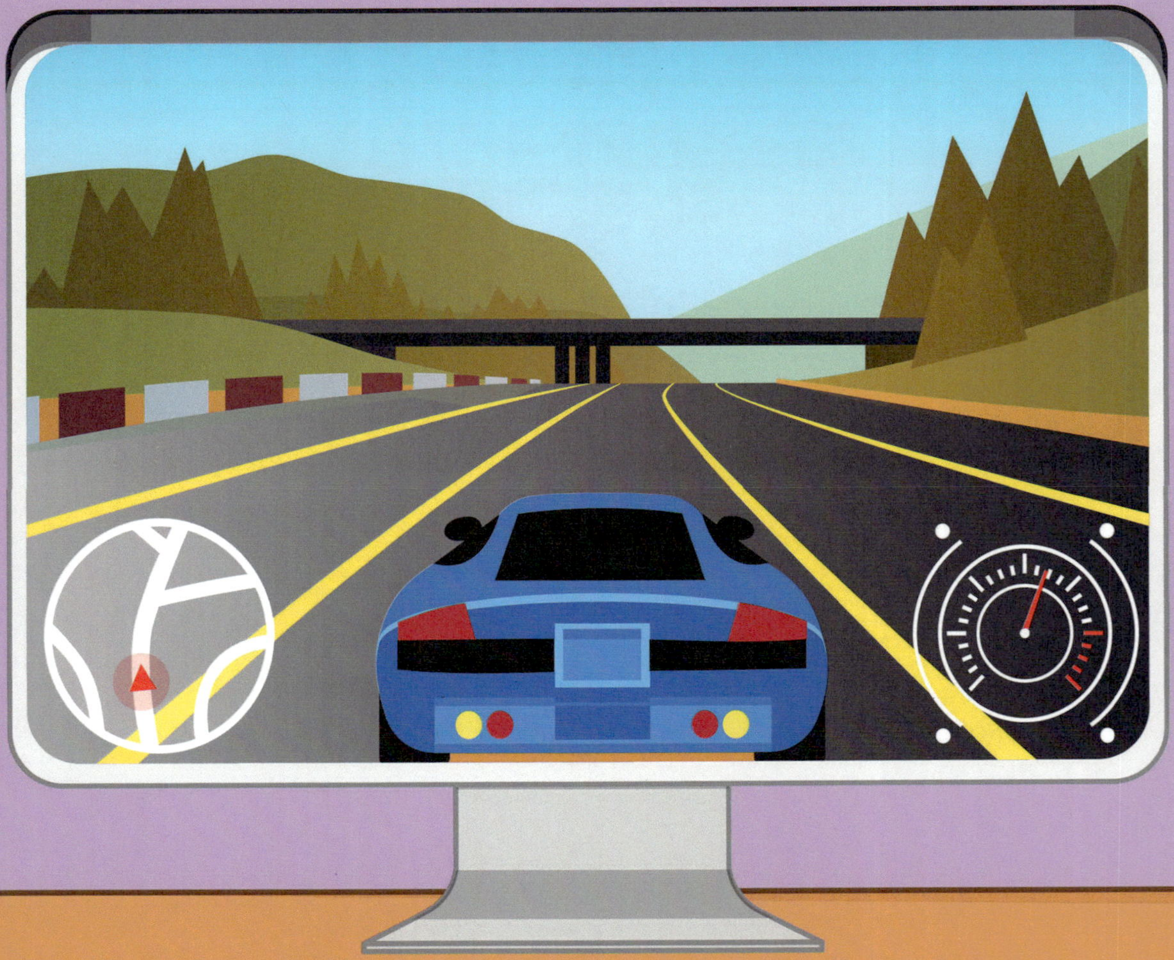

H IS FOR HARD DRIVE

Hh

A hard drive is where all of your files are stored on a computer.

Ii 

I IS FOR INTERNET

When you are online you are on the internet.

J IS FOR JOYSTICK

Jj

A joystick is used to play games on a computer.

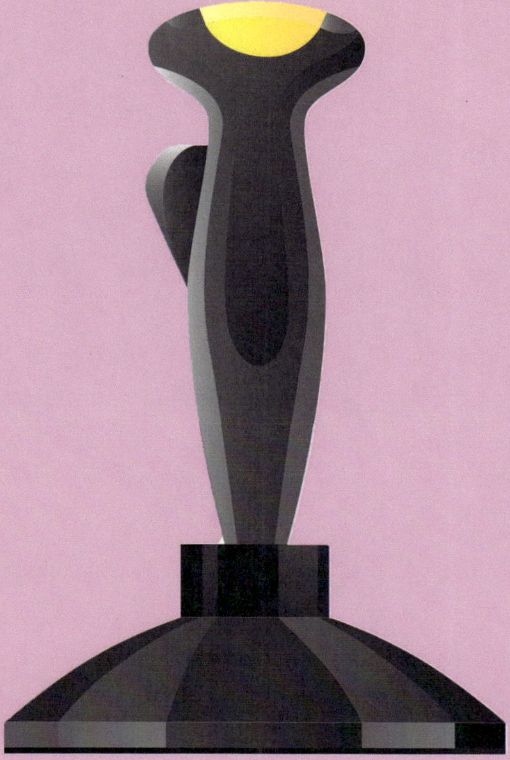

Kk

K IS FOR KEYBOARD

A keyboard allows you to type
all the letters of the alphabet.

L IS FOR LAPTOP

Ll

A laptop is a portable computer that you can take anywhere.

Mm

M IS FOR MOUSE

A computer mouse allows you to go where you want on the internet.

N IS FOR NETWORK

Nn

A computer network is a group of computers that are linked together.

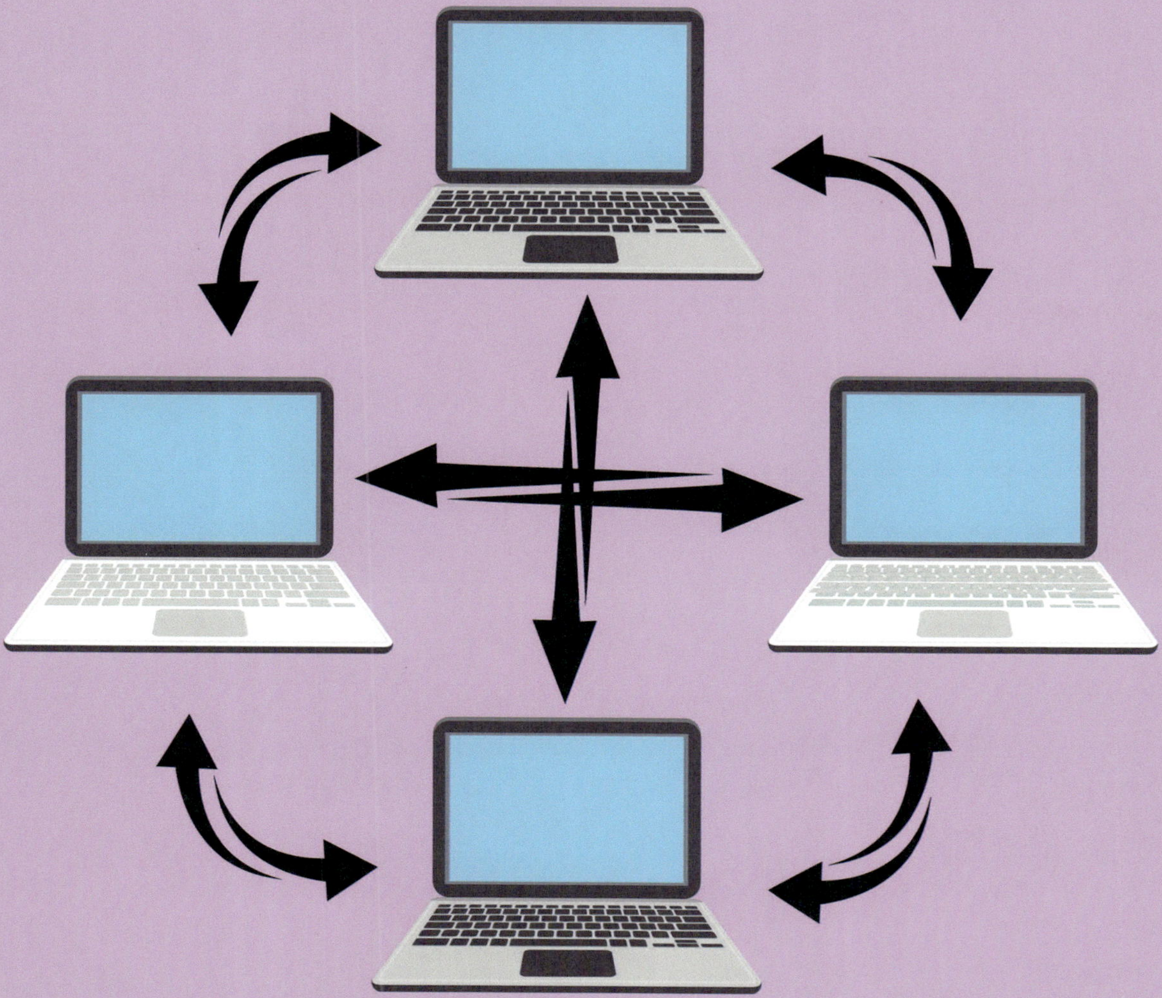

Oo 

O IS FOR ONLINE

When you are on the internet you are online.

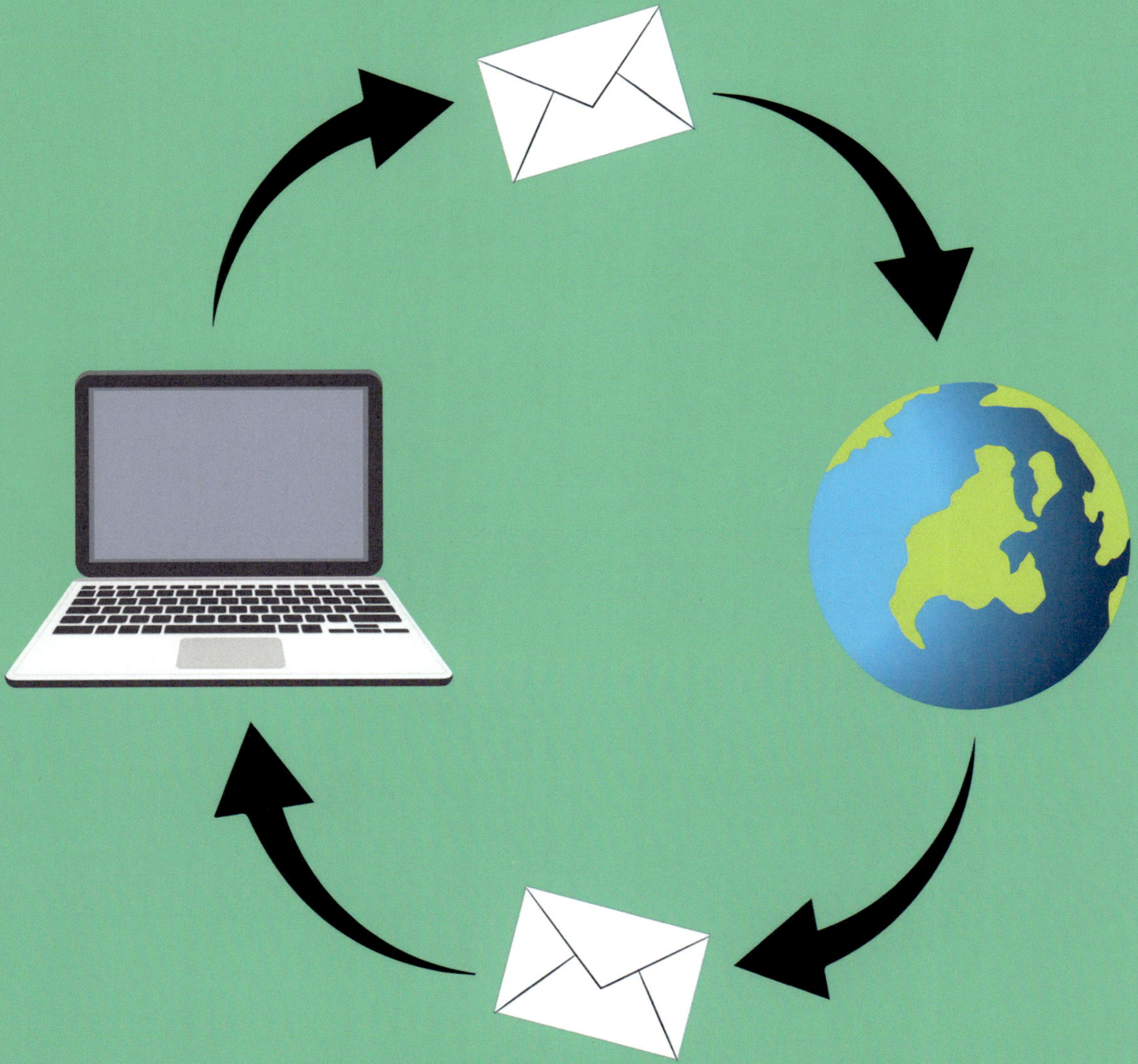

P IS FOR PRINTER

Pp

A printer can print photos or emails on paper.

Qq

Q IS FOR QUESTION

If you have a question you may find the answer online.

R IS FOR ROUTER

Rr

A router gives you a wireless connection to the internet.

Ss

S IS FOR SCREEN

You need a computer screen to see where you go online.

T IS FOR TABLET

Tt

A tablet is a touch screen computer that is portable.

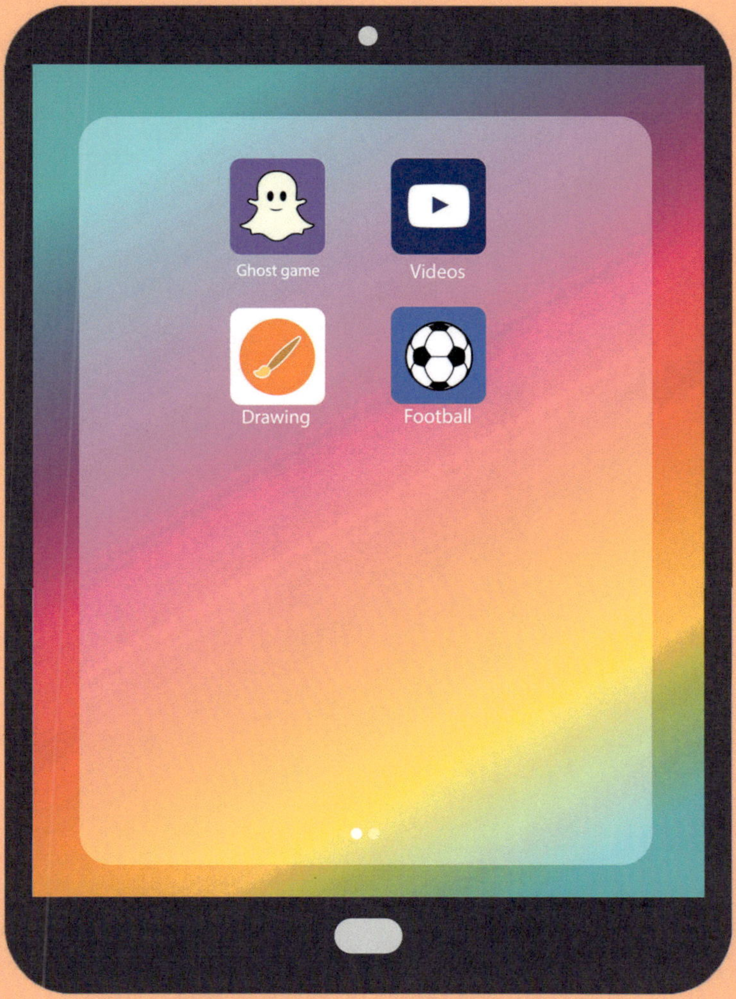

Uu

U IS FOR USB

A USB stick is a portable storage device.

V IS FOR VOLUME

Vv

You can turn the volume up or down on a computer.

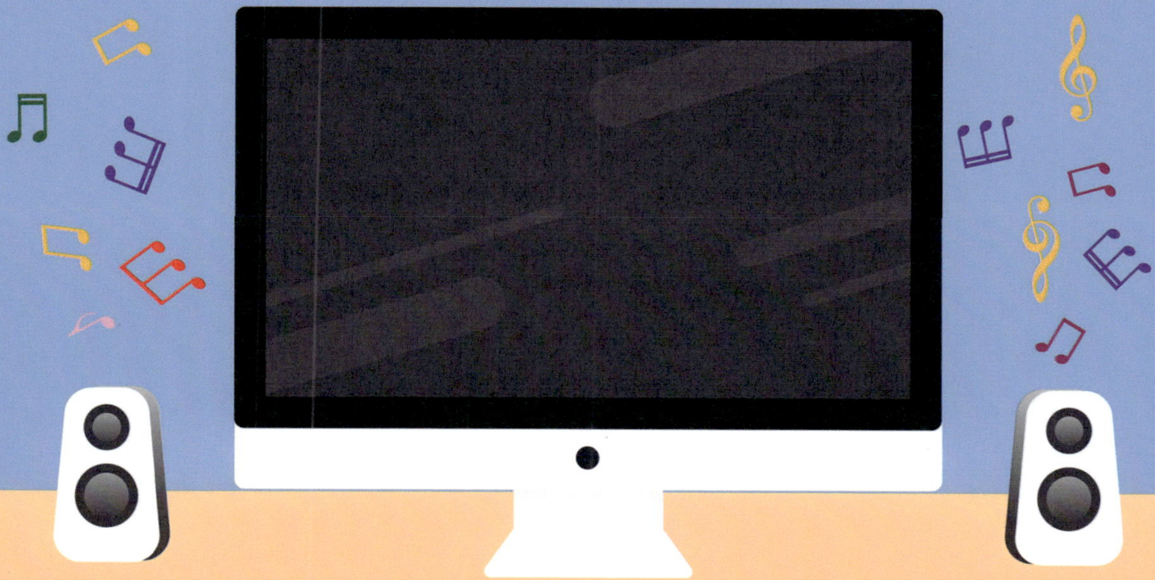

Ww

W IS FOR WEBCAM

A webcam is a camera used to see and talk to others on the internet.

X IS FOR EXIT

Xx

Click on the X to exit a webpage.

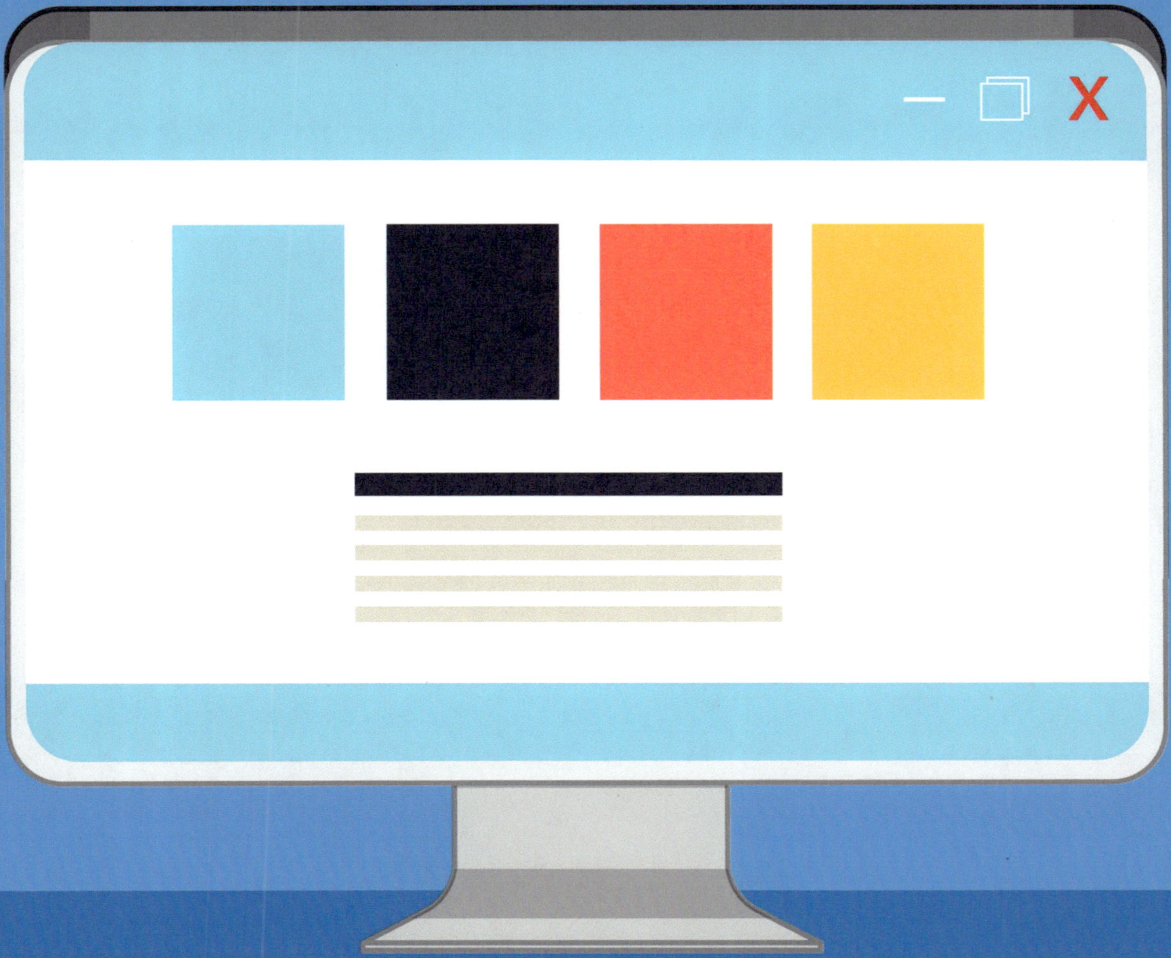

Yy

Y IS FOR YOU

You can use a computer for playing games, talking to friends and school work.

Z IS FOR ZOOM

Zz

You can zoom in on a map to see it up close.

Made in United States
Troutdale, OR
11/03/2026

56844680R00017